Walks Around the old Grain Ports
of Northumberland
Alnmouth, Seahouses and Berwick

Edited
by
Tony Barrow

Northumberland
Library

First published in 1995 by Northumberland County Library,
The Willows, Morpeth,Northumberland NE61 lTA

Printed by Pattinson and Sons, Newcastle upon Tyne

A catalogue record for this book is available from the British Library.

ISBN 1 874020 11 6

Cover photo: An unidentified brigantine, possibly the **Joanna**, lying in Alnmouth harbour c.1890.
The **Joanna** was a regular visitor to Alnmouth with cargoes of Baltic timber for the sawmill at Waterside House.
She was the last commercial sailing ship to use the harbour.
(Courtesy of Dorothy Haig).

CONTENTS

INTRODUCTION

The Northumberland coast is renowned for its sweeping sandy bays, towering medieval castles and wealth of natural life. Less well known is the long history of trade and industry on the coast, a history which has shaped the development of ports and harbours from Berwick-upon-Tweed to Seaton Sluice.

Illustrated with old photographs and plans and including detailed self-guided walks, this book explores the changing fortunes of the grain ports of Alnmouth, Seahouses and Berwick. The reader is offered a fascinating insight into the shipping and trade of the grain ports and an interpretation of their industrial archaeology.

ACKNOWLEDGEMENTS

I am grateful to Northumberland County Council for their advice and assistance in the preparation of this booklet, and to Sally Bird and Linda Bankier at Northumberland County Record Office for assistance with research and the provision of copy documents. Particular thanks are also due to Alan Glenn for detailed comments and access to his extensive collection of postcards and old photographs of Seahouses; Stuart Wilkin and Carole Grimes of Newcastle College for their copy photography and word processing skills; Adrian Osler and Dick Keyes for help and advice with illustrations.

Tony Barrow

December 1994

 Northumberland County Library acknowledges the support of the Northumberland Coast Project in the production of the three walk maps for this publication.

NORTHUMBERLAND AGRICULTURE AND THE RISE OF THE GRAIN TRADE

Agriculture has always been the most consistent and enduring characteristic of the economy of Northumberland. Despite the industrial heritage of the Northumberland coalfield, it was agriculture which sustained the employment of the majority of workers well into the nineteenth century. In the north and west of the county sheep and cattle farming was the mainstay of the local economy. By contrast, the Tyne valley and the coastal plain contained many of the county's largest arable farms. The Tweed district and the Milfield plain, to the north of Wooler, were especially important centres of cereal cultivation.

By the middle of the eighteenth century, Northumberland agriculture had entered a period of great prosperity. Enduring peace and stability in the Borders, and the economic stimulus of population growth and industrialization further south, encouraged agricultural investment. By 1800 Northumberland had developed a national reputation as a county of innovation and agricultural improvement. Farming families such as the Culley's in the north of the county, and the Grey's of Tynedale, adopted new methods and machinery to suit the needs of their own localities. They created new drainage systems, adopted horse gins for threshing cereals and experimented with the selective breeding of livestock. In the arable districts cereal cultivation soon exceeded local demand and a grain surplus became available for export to other regions.

To facilitate the movement of this grain, farmers, corn merchants and estate owners mobilised considerable amounts of capital for investment in transport improvement. During the 1750s, for example, much investment was placed in the construction of the so-called Corn Road, which ran from Hexham via the market towns of Rothbury and Alnwick, to its coastal terminus at the port of Alnmouth. One of the chief promoters of the venture was Lancelot Allgood of Nunwick, who owned a large estate in the North Tyne valley. Arable farmers were also prominent amongst those who invested in the expansion of turnpike roads in the Berwick district between 1750 and 1770, and in the construction of granaries at Alnmouth, Seahouses and Berwick after 1760. Others developed interests in shipowning. The shipping registers of Northumberland's ports abound with references to ship-owning farmers and grain merchants like John Appleby and Thomas Annett of Alnmouth, John Railston of North Sunderland and Phillip Nairn of Waren Mill.

Coastal shipping promoted a wider exchange of agricultural produce from Northumberland's farming districts than the county's more expensive road network did. However, road transport did facilitate the transfer of perishable foodstuffs to the markets of Hexham, Rothbury, Alnwick and Wooler for bulk sale and onward distribution via the Northumbrian ports.

Northumberland farm workers pose for the camera during hay making. c.1880. (Northumberland County Record Office).

In addition to their importance in the grain trade, Alnmouth and Berwick also sent a wide range of agricultural produce — butter, hams, eggs, wool-packs and leather — to more distant markets at home and abroad.

Between 1760 and 1850 the grain trade was second in importance to the coal trade in the employment of coastal shipping. As early as 1731 the ports of Berwick and Alnmouth combined to export 57,000 quarters of grain coastwise. The majority of it went to London but significant amounts also went to Scottish ports like Aberdeen, Montrose and Leith. Between 1781 and 1786 Berwick was the third most important grain port in Britain after Hull and Boston, sending 11,049 tons of grain (wheat, oats, barley and malt) coastwise. By 1819 this had more than doubled to almost 28,000 tons.

Alnmouth, Seahouses and Berwick were tidal havens, too shallow and inconvenient for large sailing ships to use, but perfectly adequate for the small vessels engaged in the grain trade. By 1830 singlemasted sloops and two-masted topsail schooners dominated the shipping types owned and operated from local ports. At Alnmouth, for example, there were ten vessels owned at the port in 1825-26; six of them were schooners, three were sloops and the other, the **Marquis of Wellington** was a brigantine. Schooners were the workhorses of the coastal trade and came to be regarded as the ideal general purpose merchant sailing ship in Britain's smaller ports. Cheap, easy to handle and good performers under certain wind conditions, an important criterion where a perishable cargo was concerned, they were ideally suited to shallow and confined harbours. The **Adventure** of Alnmouth was typical of hundreds of these ships. Built at Arbroath in 1828, this 72 ton topsail schooner usually carried a crew of five men. She was 57 feet long, 16 feet wide and could float, fully laden in about 10 feet of water. **Adventure** was purchased at Leith in 1836 for £615; each of her four owners paying £160 for a part share in the vessel including the costs of fitting her out. Schooners like the **Adventure** 'tramped' around the coastline of the British Isles and voyaged regularly to France and into the Baltic. During 1840, for example, **Adventure** completed ten voyages, called at eleven different ports from Dublin and Bangor on the west coast to Alloa, Hartlepool and Ipswich on the east, and carried grain, coal, slates and unspecified general 'goods'.

Schooners and sloops were also used in the lime trade, another important source of employment for ships during the nineteenth century. It is easy to overlook the significance that this humble commodity once had. Improvements in agricultural practices included the widespread use of lime as a means of sweetening acid soils and increasing crop yields. During his tour of Britain's agricultural regions in the 1770s, the writer

SCHEDULE (D.)

Ship _Adventure_ Of the Port of _Berwick_ whereof _H.G. Gill_ was Master

AN ACCOUNT of the VOYAGES in which the Ship _Adventure_ of _Berwick_ has been engaged in the Half Year commencing on the _First_ Day of _January_ One thousand eight hundred and _Forty_ and ending on the _Thirtieth_ Day of _June_ One thousand eight hundred and _Forty_ and of all the Persons (Master and Apprentices included) who have belonged to such Ship during that period

ACCOUNT OF THE VOYAGES.

11/320

1	Voyage Sailed Feb 7 from Alnmouth	Arrived at Grangemouth	Feb 10
2	Do Do March 8 Do	Do Senlac	March 12
3	Do Do April 9 Ipswich	Do Glasgow Dock	April 22
4	Do Do May 9 Bangor	Do Alnmouth	May 29
5	Do Do June 30 Newcastle	Do Dublin	July 12

ACCOUNT OF THE CREW.

Name.	Age.	Place of Birth	Quality.	Ship in which he last served.	Date of joining the Ship	Place where.	Time of Death or Leaving the Ship.	Place where.	How Disposed of.
H.G. Gill	31	Alnmouth	Master	Nivol	Feb 7	Alnmouth			Continued
Joseph Davison	44	Bilton	Mate	Britannia	Do	Do			Do
Jno Stanton	19	Alnmouth	Seaman	Do	Do	Do			Do
Jno Carter	24	Do	Do	Alnwick Packet	Do	Do			Do
Henry Grey	28	Do	Do	Express	March 9	Do	June 3 1840	Alnmouth	
John Rennie	12	Kinety	Apprentice		Do	Do			Continued

H.G. Gill

NOTE.—If any of the Crew shall have entered his Majesty's Service, the Name of the Queen's ship in which he entered must be stated in the Account under the head of "How Disposed of."
NOTE.—This Account is to be filled up, is to be Signed by the Owner, and deposited with the Collector or Comptroller of the Customs of the Port to which the Ship shall belong, or with the Register of Merchant Seamen in London.

A crew list of the Alnmouth schooner **Adventure** showing her voyages during the first half of 1840. She usually carried grain on her first voyage from the port and a mention of Bangor invariably meant a cargo of Welsh slates. After twenty years at the port the **Adventure** was eventually sold to Glasgow owners in 1857. (Permission of the Public Record Office).

Arthur Young noted that lime kilns were to be found throughout the crop growing districts of Northumberland. Many farms had their own lime kilns tucked away in the corner of a field or cut into a bankside. By the mid-nineteenth century large industrial lime kilns had been constructed at a number of coastal sites in north Northumberland, such as Beadnell (1798), Seahouses (1790) and Holy Island (1846 and 1860). These kilns sustained the employment of dozens of local ships, which were used to transport the lime, principally to Perth and Dundee.

But quicklime could be a volatile cargo for wooden sailing ships. There are numerous references to the loss of ships by fire when their cargo of lime ignited by spontaneous combustion after it had come into contact with sea-water. In 1868 the lime schooner **Mersey**, bound to Arbroath, sprang a leak and caught fire off Holy Island where it was beached and abandoned. Another, the **Curlew**, caught fire and sank off the May Island in the Firth of Forth. Other vessels were more fortunate and some of them appear to have had remarkably long working lives. The lime trade from the Northumberland coast was not finally abandoned until the mid 1880s. By this date the last great commercial influence on the prosperity of the old grain ports — the Herring Fishery — had come to dominate the local economy.

The growth of the North Sea Herring Fishery exerted a powerful influence on the development of Seahouses and Berwick. Indeed, sailing drifters, crowded harbour scenes and gangs of "herring girls" remain one of the most evocative images of the Northumbrian ports prior to the outbreak of the First World War. Berwick's association with the fishing industry was based initially not on herring but on the salmon fishery. Tweed salmon had been exported to the Billingsgate Fish Market in London for generations in purpose-built smacks. In their heyday these robust and seaworthy vessels were amongst the fastest sailing ships of their type anywhere on the east coast. In addition to their cargoes of grain, eggs, butter and salmon, Berwick smacks like the **Queen Charlotte** and the **King William** also ran a regular passenger service between Leith and London. In favourable conditions they could usually complete the 400 mile voyage in three days, and at two guineas for a stern cabin they were cheaper and generally more comfortable than the Edinburgh-London stagecoaches. Although the Berwick smacks were eventually challenged by steamship competition and then by the railway, a number of them were converted to schooners and continued to be employed in the coasting trade for many years. The expansion of the herring fishery provided employment for many of these ships which were commonly owned by coopers and fish-curers at Tweedmouth, Spittal and Berwick.

The outbreak of the First World War marked the end of an era. By 1914 the grain trade had all but disappeared from the

Northumbrian ports and the herring fishery, which had reached a peak of prosperity before the war, declined rapidly after the loss of the German and Russian markets. Nowadays only Berwick maintains an association with the grain trade. Small coasters still load Northumberland barley at the Tweed Dock, principally for the whisky distilleries of the Western Isles and the breweries of Southern England. In 1983 the European Community provided a grant of £200,000 towards the maintenance of grain silos and loading facilities and thereby secured the immediate future of this traditional export trade.

Modern Seahouses is also a working harbour which attracts thousands of visitors every year. In addition to its small fleet of fishing vessels, numerous day boats cater for the tourist trade and ferry thousands of people to the Farne Islands during the summer months. Few of these visitors are aware that around the old harbour and behind the main streets, there are numerous traces of a byegone age when Seahouses bustled with the activities of a different kind of visitor — herring 'girls' from Shetland, fishermen from Cornwall and the Channel Islands and merchant seamen from Western Ireland or the Baltic.

By contrast, the old grain port of Alnmouth never attracted the herring boats, and was too shallow and inconvenient for steamships to use. The growth of Amble and the arrival of the Newcastle and Berwick railway in 1850, gradually eroded the remaining trade of the port. Although grain continued to be shipped from Alnmouth until the 1860s and the saw mill at Waterside House received cargoes of Baltic timber until the 1890s, shipping movements became infrequent and the harbour decayed. Most of the granaries had been converted to other uses by 1914, but they remain the most distinctive feature of the industrial archaeology of Alnmouth and stand as testimony to the importance the grain trade once had at this ... "small seaport town, famous for all kinds of wickedness" ... (John Wesley's Journal, 1748).

ALNMOUTH AND ALNMOUTH HARBOUR

By Tony Barrow

INTRODUCTION

Alnmouth experienced many phases of growth and decline after its foundation in the Middle Ages but enjoyed its greatest period of prosperity during the eighteenth century. In 1730 Alnmouth was described as ... "a very good harbour for ships and a flourishing place for trade" ... The Corn Road and the construction of a number of large granaries after 1750 consolidated the prosperity of the port. In addition to the export of grain and other agricultural products, Alnmouth also served as the principal entrepot of mid-Northumberland. Return cargoes commonly included soft soap, fullers earth and allum which were used in the local woollen industry and few ships arrived from London without a quantity of wine, spirits, beer and tobacco. By contrast, in the mid-nineteenth century, Alnmouth became an important distribution point for Baltic timber and Peruvian guano. Alnmouth last hosted a commercial sailing ship in 1896 and the harbour has silted considerably since then. However, the port still retains many of the characteristics which would have been familiar to the seamen of the Victorian era.

* The walk begins from the Boathouses Car Park on Alnmouth Links. It is marked No. 1 on your map.

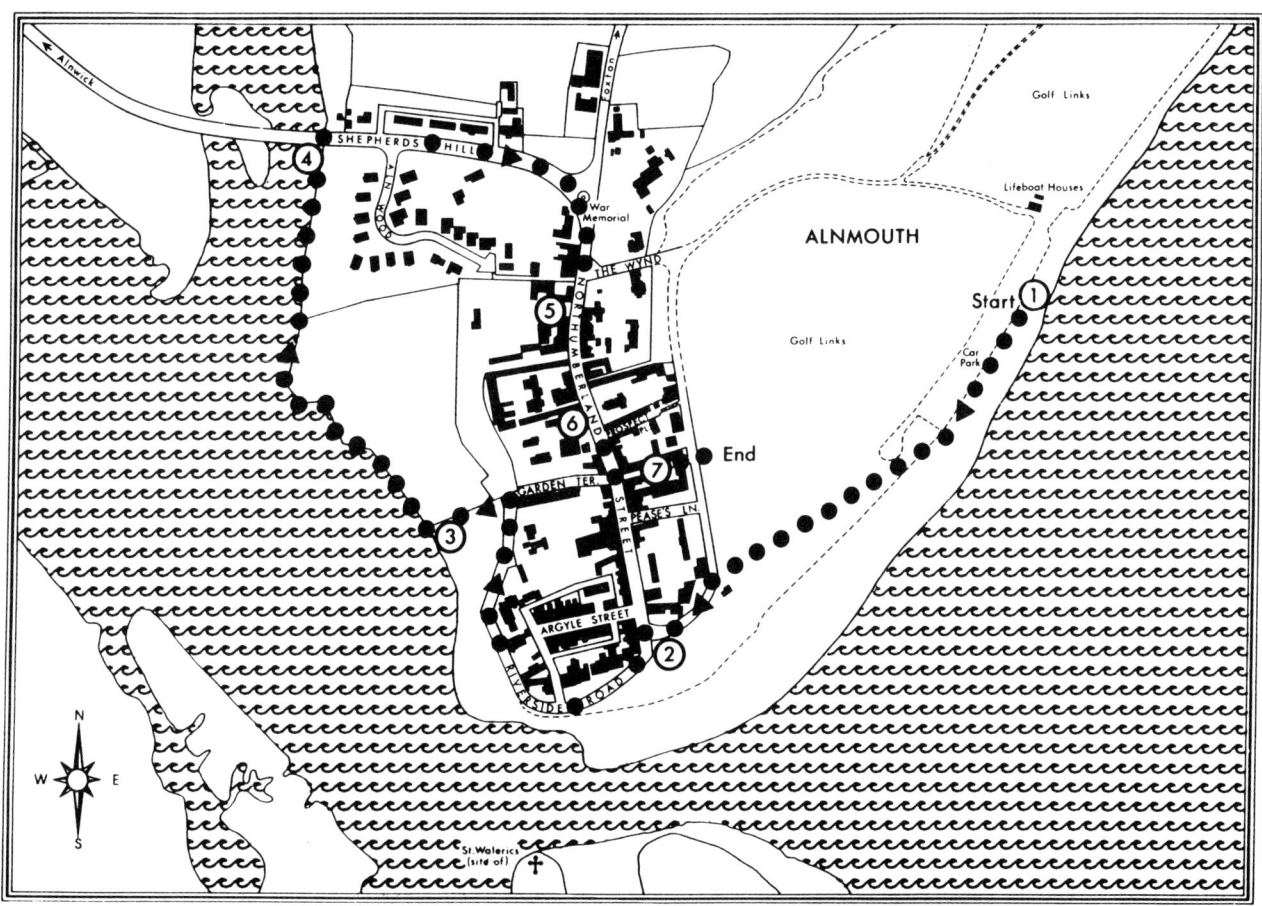

Guide map for walk

(© Crown Copyright)

13

THE BOATHOUSES AND THE OLD BATTERY

The Boathouses were built in the mid-nineteenth century. The first lifeboat was provided by the Duke of Northumberland about 1850. The second was donated by the Pease family sometime later and used specifically for the protection and rescue of bathers who flocked to Alnmouth during the summer months after the arrival of the railway.

On the high ground behind the Boathouses are the remains of the Old Battery, constructed at the expense of the Duke of Northumberland and completed in March 1881. It was altered substantially during World War Two to accommodate heavy coastal defence guns. The beacon behind the Battery was erected in 1988 to commemorate the 400th anniversary of the sighting of the Spanish Armada. It was the 428th beacon in a chain which ended at Berwick-upon-Tweed.

ALNMOUTH COMMON

Alnmouth Common lies between the Boathouses Car Park and Marine Road. During the Middle Ages it was used by the burgesses for grazing livestock. As the trade of the port developed during the eighteenth century Alnmouth Common was used for the storage of the construction materials — Welsh slates, pantiles, bricks and timber — carried into Alnmouth as return cargoes. The old photograph of Alnmouth shows this very clearly. Taken about 1870, it shows a brigantine aground at the harbour mouth, and between it and Marine Road miscellaneous stocks of tiles and timber. At the left centre of the photograph what appears to be a small crane stands beside a large saw pit and in the centre of the photograph the Hindmarsh Hall, a former granary, rises above the rooftops of the buildings on Marine Road.

The 9-hole Golf Course on the Common was laid out for the Alnmouth Working Mens Golf Club in 1869 and is the second oldest links course in the country.

* From the Car Park follow the coastal path towards the river mouth. The path joins Marine Road close to the old Coastguard Station which is now part of the Golf Club. There are some public toilets on the opposite side of the road. Make your way up the hill to the junction with Northumberland Street. It is marked No. 2 on your map.

CHURCH HILL AND THE HARBOUR ENTRANCES

Church Hill with its wooden cross dedicated to St Cuthbert is Alnmouth's most prominent landmark. Local tradition claims that Alnmouth is the Twyford mentioned in Bede's

A view across Alnmouth Common about 1870. A brigantine discharges its cargo at the harbour entrance. Notice the long axis of the old granaries in Prospect Place and the absence of the spire of the Parish Church, which was not consecrated until 1876. (Courtesy of Dorothy Haig).

Ecclesiastical History as the place where Cuthbert was chosen to be Bishop of Lindisfarne in 684 A.D. The original church was a Saxon foundation which was probably destroyed by the Vikings during the ninth century. In 1789 the shaft of a carved stone cross dating to the Saxon period was discovered at the foot of Church Hill. A second, Norman church was constructed on the site during the twelfth century. It was a substantial building in the Romanesque style but its position made it vulnerable to coastal erosion. The church was already a ruin by the early 18th century although the graveyard continued to be used for another century. In 1870 the Victorians constructed a mortuary chapel on the west side of Church Hill.

Church Hill was eventually cut off from the rest of the village by a great storm which arose on Christmas Day, 1806. The sea burst through the sand dunes and altered the course of the River Aln to form the harbour entrance that you see today. Before 1806 the channel of the river passed to the south around the back of Church Hill. It is still possible to trace the course of this old channel, low down to the left at the foot of Church Hill as you look. Parts of the old channel still flood at Spring tides. Another clue is the derelict, barn-like building in the distance beyond Church Hill. This 18th century structure stood on the south side of the old river channel and was used to store imported guano in the 19th century. Guano was widely used as a fertiliser by local farmers but its appalling smell demanded that it was stored as far as possible from the inhabitants of the town. Eighteenth century maps of Alnmouth also indicate the sites of several granaries on the south side of the harbour.

NAVIGATION AND SHIPPING

It is often stated that the alteration of the harbour entrance in 1806 led to the decline of Alnmouth as a commercial port because it made the river more susceptible to silting. This is clearly untrue, indeed the new entrance was probably better because it was shorter and straighter than the old one. Ships approaching the harbour would usually enter at high water with the last of the floodtide. Sometimes they were hauled or walked into the harbour in calm weather. If wind and tide proved unfavourable then ships would partially discharge their cargoes before attempting to enter the port. Of course, there was always the usual crop of casualties. In August 1835 the **Good Agreement** inward bound for Littlehampton grounded at the harbour entrance, but refloated and entered the harbour on the next high tide without damage. Local ships were just as susceptible to these accidents as strangers were. In December 1835 the **Marquis of Wellington**, a brigantine owned and operated from Alnmouth, stuck on the harbour bar when outward bound with grain and suffered considerable damage. Part of the cargo had to be discharged before the **Marquis of Wellington** could get back into the port for repairs. Incidents such as these were commonplace in the age of sail. In 1841 the rates of insurance for shipping using the Tyne, Seaton Sluice, Blyth, Amble and Alnmouth were exactly the same — 7/6d (37½p) for every £100 of value of the ship, cargo or both.

HINDMARSH HALL

Turning from the harbour entrance and Church Hill cross the road to Victoria Place. These neat stone-built cottages were originally built in the late seventeenth or early eighteenth century. No. 1 on the left of the terrace was originally the Seven Stars Inn, one of Alnmouth's numerous public houses during the eighteenth century. Behind Victoria Place on Northumberland Street is the Hindmarsh Hall, named after one of the principal merchant/shipowning families of Alnmouth who purchased the Hall in the 1930s. This impressive building was constructed as a granary in the eighteenth century and is probably the earliest and most prominent of Alnmouth's surviving granaries. Buttressed walls and blocked granary openings are evidence of its former use. It ceased to be used as a granary about 1850, but was converted to serve as the Corn Exchange and then remodelled

and used as an Anglican Chapel until the new parish church replaced it in 1876. The Hindmarsh Hall has been used as a meeting room and village hall ever since.

* Retrace your path and make your way along Riverside Road to the point marked No. 3 on your map. You will pass the Old Ferry steps half way down the hill and then the Ferry hut. Both are reminders that it was possible at one time to take a ferryboat across to Church Hill. Continue past Pease's Park, the children's playground on your left, to the point where Riverside Road meets Garden Terrace. Take the footpath on the left and walk to the point marked No. 3.

ALNMOUTH HARBOUR AND ITS TRADE

Viewed from here the natural harbour of Alnmouth has changed little over the centuries. The trade of the port and the types of vessels commonly using it did not require significant investment in harbour improvement. The Duke of Northumberland undertook to provide and maintain a number of mooring posts, called dolphins, in return for a charge of one shilling (5p) per ship. The remains of two of these mooring posts can still be seen on the foreshore close to the Ferryman's hut, and others are revealed from time to time towards the centre of the harbour. You are standing on part of the old

*The old brigantine **Peace**, built at Yarmouth in 1801, discharging her cargo of timber at Alnmouth c.1875. (Northumberland County Record Office).*

harbour wall and on the hill to your left there is a brick-built tower-like structure which was formerly used as a watchtower and the harbour master's office. It is an early eighteenth century building and stands in the grounds of the Grange, another of Alnmouth's converted granaries, which can be seen to the right of the tower behind the trees. Looking south from this point it is also possible to see the ruins of the Mortuary Chapel on the western side of Church Hill.

In the late eighteenth century it was not unusual to find ten or more ships in the harbour together. Most of them carried grain coastwise to Newcastle, Leith and London, others were involved in the export trade to Europe. In July 1771, for example, ten vessels sailed from the port with grain. They included, on 6 July, the **Brotherly Love** and the **William** for Newcastle with wheat, and on 8 July the **Isabella** and the **Janet** for Leith with 480 quarters (72 tons) of oats. Another vessel, the **Greta and Ann** sailed for Bergen on the same day, probably on the same high tide that witnessed the arrival of the **Hopewell and Providence** (Captain Young) from London. She was carrying a mixed cargo of fullers earth, salt petre, tin plate, tea, sugar, oranges, lemons, rum and beer. Other ships like the **Alnwick Packet** brought cargoes of timber, Russian iron and barrels of tar. Waterside House across on the western side of the harbour was the site of a saw-mill which continued to receive cargoes of Baltic timber well into the nineteenth century.

* From this point follow the footpath along the old harbour wall. It turns west and north again before it reaches a small coppice which projects into the estuary. This is known as Pan Leazes and, as its name suggests, was once the site of several salt pans. Salt was mentioned as one of the commodities exported from Alnmouth during the 1720s. Continue along the riverside as far as the Duchess Bridge. It is marked No. 4 on your map.

THE DUCHESS BRIDGE

The arrival of the railway was a mixed blessing for Alnmouth. On the one hand it hastened the decline of the port but on the other it led to the development of Alnmouth as a resort. However, direct access from the railway station was difficult and the Corn Road from Lesbury was a long and roundabout route. To overcome this problem a temporary wooden bridge was constructed about 1850. It proved to be an immediate success ... "the traffic along the bridge is very great" ... wrote a contemporary observer in the Alnwick Journal on January 15, 1864 ... "consisting chiefly of timber, slates, guano, corn and coals ..." There was also a constant stream of visitors especially during the summer months when it was not uncommon to find 500 people arriving at Alnmouth station on a single train to enjoy a day at the seaside. In January 1864 it was decided to raise a subscription to reconstruct the bridge in stone. The estimated cost of the new bridge, £650, was soon raised and the Duchess Bridge was completed before the end of the year.

* Now make your way up Shepherd's Hill past the Methodist Church of 1891 and turn right at the War Memorial Roundabout. You have now joined the old Corn Road where it entered Alnmouth from Lesbury. Walk past Alnmouth Working Men's Club to the point marked No. 5 on your map.

THE HALL AND HALLSTEADS

In its heyday Alnmouth possessed a number of leading citizens who accumulated considerable wealth from their association with granaries and the grain trade. The Gallon's owned a great deal of land in Alnmouth as did the Gibb, Wilkinson and Hindmarsh families. Many of the houses that they built, together with their associated granaries, still survive. The Hall and Hallsteads are both eighteenth century buildings although they look very different to each other. The Hall is the brick-built building on the left. It was substantially altered during the nineteenth century when the peculiar tower was added. Hallsteads once incorporated a granary and the garden wall that surrounds it reveals an interesting blocked doorway with a lintel inscribed T^L_A 1713.

THE BURGAGES

Alnmouth was a planned medieval town and still retains its distinctive form. As you walk down Northumberland Street to the next stopping point notice the way in which the adjoining lanes run at right angles from the main street. These lanes indicate the boundaries of the medieval burgages. Their owners, or burgesses, usually built their dwellings and granaries at the point where the burgage strip joined the main street. This explains why there are so many gable ends fronting onto Northumberland Street with the long axis of the buildings at right angles to it. Grosvenor Terrace and the Sun Inn Public House on your right are good examples. Crows Nest Lane on the opposite side of the road is another.

* Continue as far as the Red Lion Public House on the right hand side of Northumberland Street. It is marked No. 6 on your map.

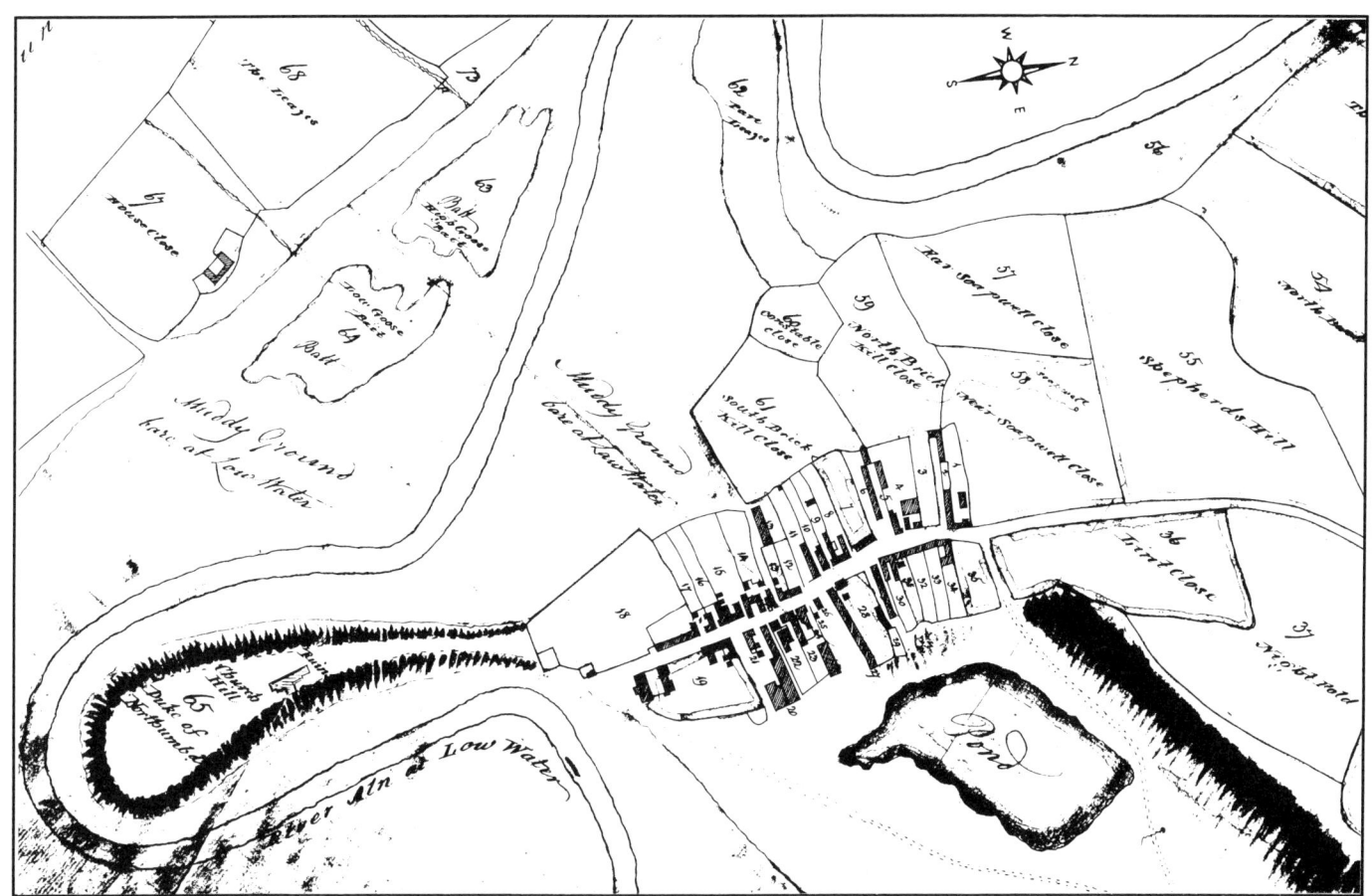

Estate plan of Alnmouth 1802. (Northumberland County Record Office).

THE PARISH CHURCH AND PROSPECT PLACE GRANARY

The church of St John the Baptist was built to replace the Hindmarsh Hall which served as an Anglican Chapel from 1859-76. It was built in a simple 13th century style and was consecrated as the parish church of Alnmouth in 1876.

The building to the right of the church, in Prospect Place, is perhaps the most obvious example of an eighteenth century granary conversion in Alnmouth. The rear of the building facing the churchyard, displays a number of small sash windows and numerous blocked openings which suggest its former use. Cross the road to Prospect Place, which is another burgage strip, and take time to look at the fabric of the building. There are numerous blocked openings and alterations in the stonework. Notice particularly the stone external stair to a blocked doorway on the first floor of No. 8 Prospect Place. All the small upper windows have been built into original eighteenth century openings. The roof is Welsh slate which was a common return cargo for the Alnmouth schooners and was used extensively in the district. Some of the residents of Prospect Place have examples of barley and other grains recovered from behind the lath and plaster internal walls and one of the houses retains a grain shoot used to deliver corn from the upper floors of the granary. At the eastern end of

Prospect Place beside a flight of stairs is another eighteenth century granary. It was converted to a vicarage in the nineteenth century and is now the Marine House Hotel.

* Return along Prospect Place and turn left into Northumberland Street. Notice the attractive brick-built Aln House of 1740 on the opposite side of the road and Garden Terrace, another burgage. It was originally called Salters Lane. Further down Northumberland Street on the right is the Schooner Inn, one of Alnmouth's oldest and best known public houses. Turn left into Chapel Lane and walk to the point marked No. 7 on your map.

WESLEYAN CHAPEL

Chapel Lane marks the boundary of another burgage. As you walk towards the chapel notice the date 1727 on the lintel above the door of one of the cottages. The end cottage has a buttressed wall which may suggest that it served as a small granary at one time. The old Wesleyan Chapel on the left was built about 1750 and is one of the earliest of its type. It was used for meetings until the opening of the Wesleyan Church on Shepherd's Hill in 1891. Notice the cross set into the wall opposite the chapel. It commemorates John Wesley's visit to Alnmouth in 1748. He is reputed to have delivered an open air sermon to the citizens of Alnmouth close to this spot.

* Walk to the foot of Chapel Lane where it meets Marine Road and Alnmouth Common.

Your walk around the old port of Alnmouth ends here. However, there are a number of other walks and places of interest in the locality. You might like to consider the following suggestions.

1. Find your way to the south side of Alnmouth Harbour and explore Church Hill, the old river channel and the guano sheds.

2. Visit the historic town and castle of Alnwick which is only a short drive away.

3. Move on to Walk 2 described in this book — Seahouses and North Sunderland Harbour.

SEAHOUSES AND NORTH SUNDERLAND HARBOUR

By David Bond

INTRODUCTION

Although the natural harbour at North Sunderland had been used by local fishermen for centuries it was the development of lime burning and the export of grain that stimulated the development of the harbour. In February 1768 the Lord Crewe Trustees granted a seven year lease to John Pringle and James Blackett permitting them to quarry limestone at North Sunderland Snook. They were also given permission to mine local coal seams and export lime from the harbour. Seahouses developed rapidly as a result and by 1841 it was a prosperous community of over 1000 inhabitants. In 1843-44 there were over 250 separate shipping movements through the port, principally of lime traders and vessels engaged in carrying grain and herring. A new harbour, completed in 1888, and the arrival of the railway ten years later consolidated the prosperity of Seahouses which remained a regular port of call for the herring fleets until after the Second World War.

* The walk begins at the Tourist Information Office marked No. 1 on your map.

THE NORTH SUNDERLAND RAILWAY

The modern car park occupies the site of the Seahouses terminus of the North Sunderland Railway. It was constructed between 1896-98 as a branch railway to the east coast main line at Chathill. Work on the railway commenced on 21 May, 1896 and opened to freight trains on 1 August, 1898. The first passenger train ran the four miles to Chathill on 14 December, 1898 ... "free to all who felt inclined for a trip". The construction of the railway reflected the great prosperity that the herring fleets had brought to Seahouses. It also contributed significantly to the development of the tourist trade. Unfortunately, despite the confidence of its promoters, the North Sunderland Railway was never a profitable line and it was eventually closed in October 1951.

* From the car park cross the main road and walk to the new lifeboat house. It is marked No. 2 on your map. Visitors are welcome to look at the exhibits inside and view one of the RNLI's modern Mersey-class lifeboats.

NORTH SUNDERLAND LIFEBOAT

The stretch of coast between Seahouses and Bamburgh has been associated with lifeboats since the end of the eighteenth century. There has been a lifeboat stationed at North Sunderland since 1827. The present lifeboat, the **Grace Darling**, commemorates the name of one of the best known heroines of the Victorian age. Grace was only twenty three

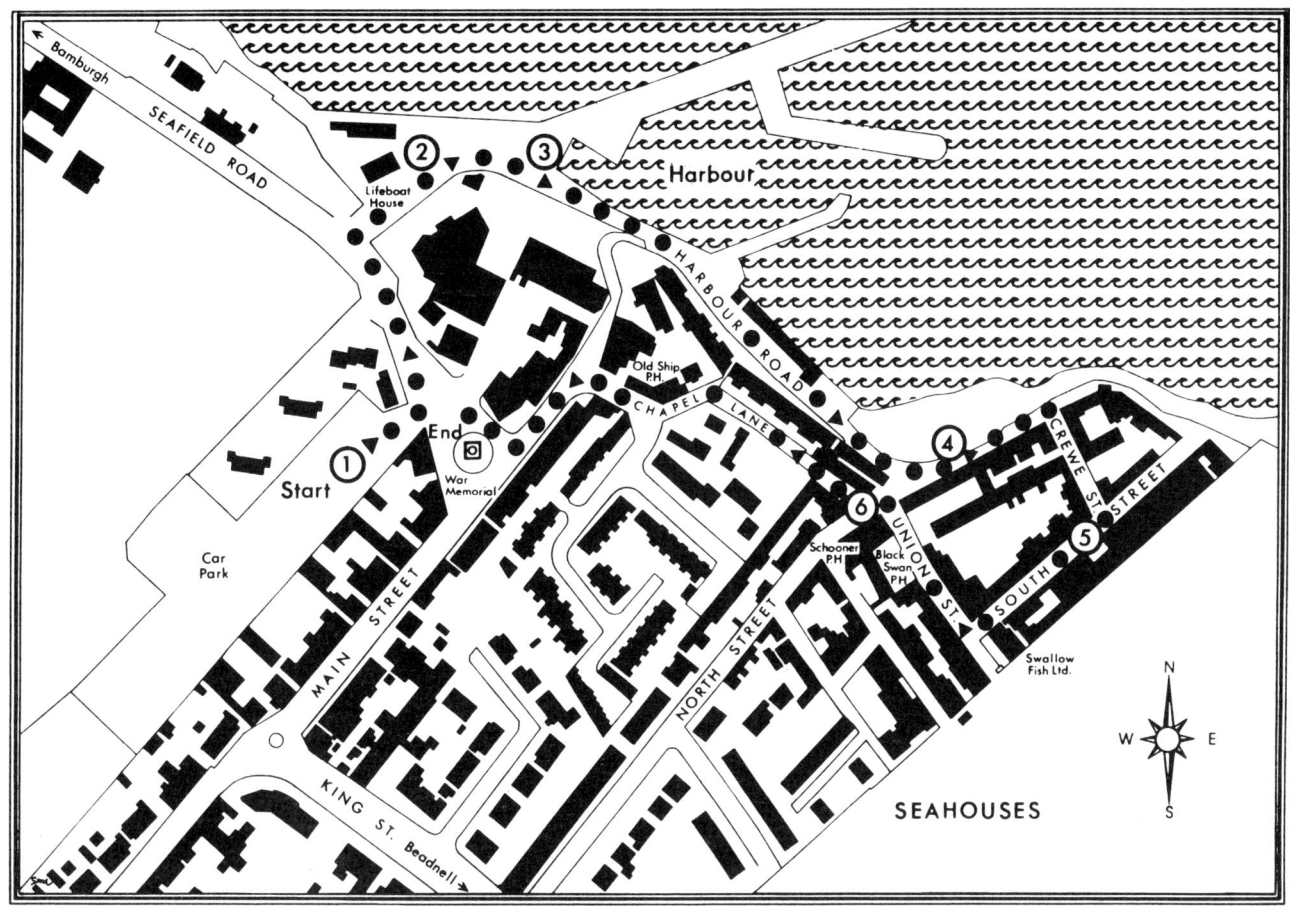

Guide map for walk

years old when she assisted her father William Darling, Keeper of the Longstone Lighthouse, in the rescue of nine survivors from the wreck of the **Forfarshire** in 1838. That famous shipwreck is only the most well known of a countless number that have occurred on this stretch of the coast.

* From the lifeboat house walk down the hill to the harbour and view the limekilns from the point marked No. 3 on your map.

THE LIMEKILNS AND THE OLD QUAY

The limekilns at Seahouses together with others at Beadnell and Holy Island are amongst the most impressive examples of industrial archaeology in the North of England. The quarrying and burning of limestone was an important industry at Seahouses for almost a century. The kilns, constructed during the 1770s, consist of seven combustion chambers or "pots" which were used in the manufacture of quicklime. The kilns were charged with limestone and coal in the ratio of approximately 5:1 at the top of the combustion chambers and were able to generate temperatures in excess of 1000°C. After roasting, the lime fell to the base of the kiln where it was raked from the draw arches, allowed to cool, and then loaded into sailing ships waiting at the old quay.

THE LIME TRADERS

The majority of vessels engaged in the lime trade carried their cargoes to Scotland, principally to Perth and Dundee. Most of them were sloops ranging in size from the diminutive **Rachel**, 32 tons, to the 68 ton **Archduke** which was owned and registered at Dundee. The lime trade from Seahouses seems to have peaked during the 1830s and 1840s when vessels sailed from the harbour almost every day during the summer months. Each ship could usually complete two round voyages per month during a season which began in March and ended in October or November. Despite the volatile nature of their cargoes many of these lime traders had remarkably long working lives. The **Hannah** worked from Seahouses for over 40 years, until 1867, when she foundered near Berwick with the loss of everyone on board. Others like the **Belford** and the **Robert Hood** continued to carry lime from the jetty at Holy Island after the closure of the kilns at Seahouses in about 1860.

* Now walk along the old quay and follow the harbour road to a point above the harbour where there are a number of public seats. It is marked No. 4 on your map.

THE OLD HARBOUR AND THE GRANARIES

There are, in fact, 3 harbours here at North Sunderland; a natural harbour with the original quay wall, now largely hidden by subsequent building; the old harbour constructed by Robert Crammond during the 1780s and the new harbour built between 1886 and 1887 to accommodate the increasing number of herring drifters landing their catches at the port. The old harbour follows the line of Harbour Road from the lime kilns and includes the stone piers which enclose the inner basin where most of the fishing boats are tied up. Parts of the old harbour wall can still be seen, partially buried in the sand of the small beach. A closer inspection will reveal the remains of some iron mooring rings. After the construction of the inner harbour it was used as the fish quay. The line of buildings at the south end of Harbour Road, which are now used as holiday flats, were originally constructed as granaries. They are the only survivors of the ... "six commodious granaries ..." advertised to let in the local newspapers in January 1821. They were converted to dwellings during the second half of the nineteenth century and so thoroughly modernized during the 1970s that very little of their original fabric now survives.

THE GRAIN TRADERS

Although it was never as important as Berwick and Alnmouth, the harbour at North Sunderland was used for the shipment of considerable quantities of corn. In 1846-47 thirty one vessels carried 7447 quarters, more than 1000 tons, of grain from the

Two schooners load herring at Seahouses while in the foreground some local fishermen secure their boats after a day's fishing c1890. (Courtesy of Alan Glenn).

port. The principal corn merchant was John Railston who owned and operated several vessels including the **John**, a 69 ton schooner, the **Beadnell** and the aptly named **Constant Trader** which worked from Seahouses during the 1830s. Their return cargoes commonly included salt, barrel staves and iron hoops for the herring curers as well as bricks, tiles and timber. John Railston's house and granary can still be seen in North Sunderland village.

THE NEW HARBOUR

The old harbour at North Sunderland was extended during the 1880s by the addition of the north pier and the construction of the east breakwater. Most of the work was financed by the Lord Crewe Trustees and completed in 1888 at a cost of £31,000. In addition to fleets of herring boats, which crowded into the harbour between July and September, small steamers and Baltic schooners were also regular visitors to Seahouses before the First World War. Most of them loaded herring for Hamburg, Danzig and St Petersburg, and were sometimes so heavily laden that they had difficulty getting out of the harbour. On 6 October, 1892, the Harbour Master, George Tait, recorded in his Journal the experience of one German sailing ship, the **Clara Deakleman** ... "This ship was drawing twelve feet of water" ... he wrote ... "[and] a great deal of difficulty

was experienced in getting her out. After breaking all of his ropes we were obliged to take two pair of horses and with about thirty men at the capstan succeeded in getting her to sea..." Another German Schooner, the **Bertha,** arrived to load herrings on the following day but had no difficulty in getting to sea with her cargo.

THE FARNE ISLANDS

Beyond the harbour, to the north and north east, there is a panoramic view to Bamburgh Castle, Lindisfarne and out to the Farne Islands. The Chapel of St Cuthbert on Inner Farne was extensively restored in the nineteenth century but retains some medieval masonry in the north wall. The interior contains some richly decorated seventeenth century woodwork made for Bishop Cosin at Durham Cathedral and brought to the chapel in the 1840s. The lighthouse and keeper's cottage were built in 1809-10 for Trinity House, Newcastle. The stump of a second lighthouse of the same date on Brownsman Island is visible between Inner Farne and the Longstone. The famous lighthouse on Longstone was built in 1826.

The Farne Islands represent one of the principal dangers to navigation on the east coast of Britain and were notorious in the age of sail. On 2 February, 1823 William Darling wrote in

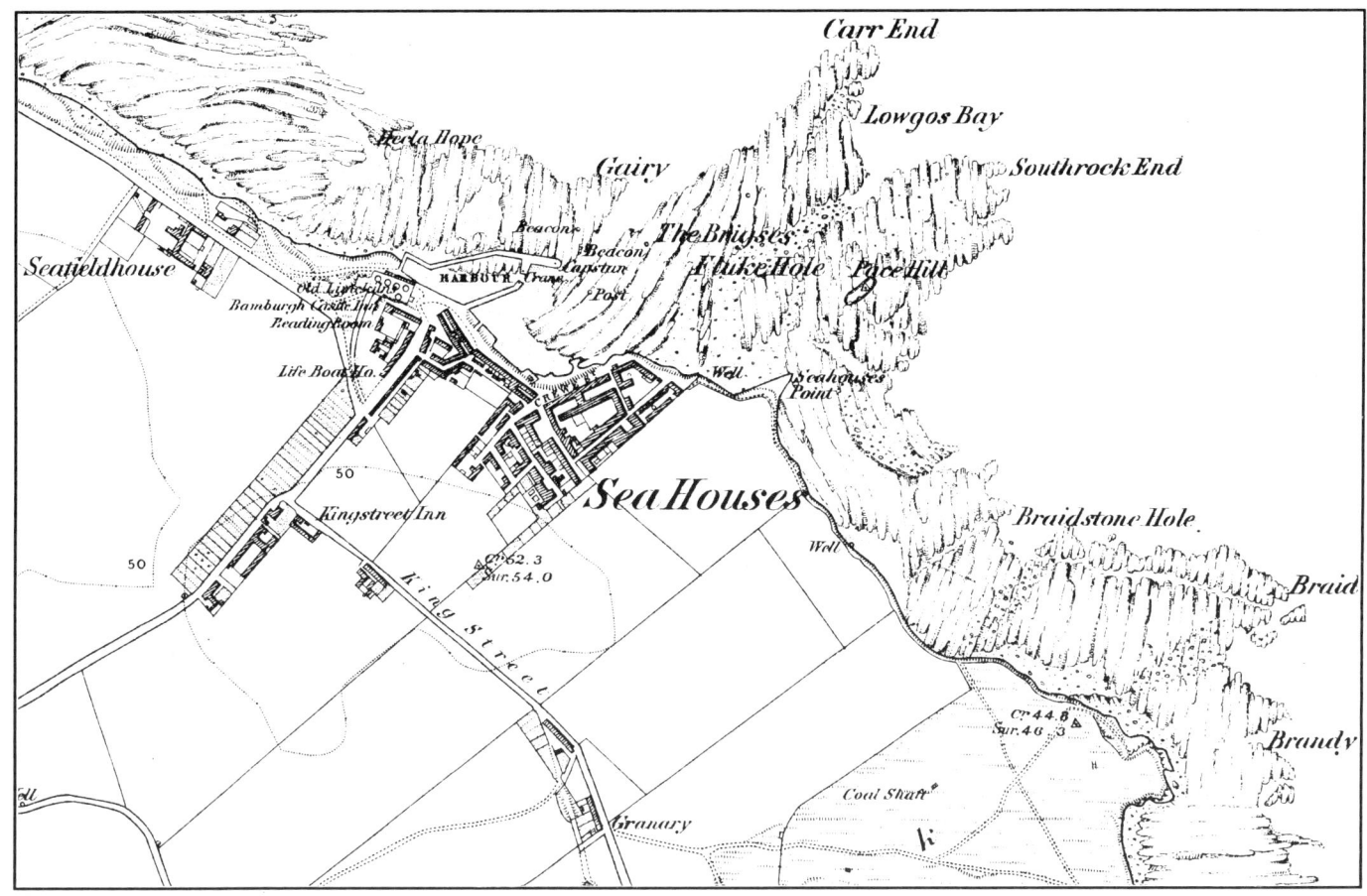

Carr End

Lowgos Bay

Herla Hope

Southrock End

Gairy

The Brigges

Beacon

Fluke Hole

Pace Hill

Beacon
Capstan
Post

Seahouses

HARBOUR

Crane

Old Lifeboat

Seafieldhouse

Bamburgh Castle Inn
Reading Room

Life Boat Ho.

Well

Seahouses
Point

50

Braidstone Hole

Kingstreet Inn

Well

Braid

Cr 62.3
Sur 54.0

50

King Street

Brandy

Cr 44.8
Sur 46.3

H

Coal Shaft

Granary

h

Seahouses, 1860

(Reproduced from the 1860 Ordnance Survey Map)

A Fraserburgh registered fishing boat leaves Seahouses harbour. Scenes like this were commonplace before the First World War. (Courtesy of Alan Glenn).

his journal .."Severe gale, east, snow storm. The **George and Mary**, brigantine, 11½ keels coal load, for London, struck the east point of Brownsman Island and became a total wreck. All hands perished. About the same time, 8 p.m. H.W., the **Fortitude** brigantine, 13 keels coal load, totally lost on Grahamstone and all hands perished. Also the **Augusta** brigantine, 12 keels supposed to have struck the rocks near Holy Island and all hands perished. The **Mermaid**, **Active** and **Lucia and Charlotte** got onto Bamburgh sands ... all hands saved"...

* Walk to the end of Crewe Street and turn right. Follow the street to its junction with South Street. Notice the courtyard on Sunnieside Square on your right as you make your way to Craster Square which is marked No. 5 on your map.

CHINATOWN AND THE FISHERMEN'S SQUARES

This part of Seahouses is known locally as Chinatown, possibly because it was the most densely populated area of the village during the nineteenth century. The arrangement of the fishermen's cottages around three sides of a courtyard was typical of many fishing communities on the east coast. The open courtyard was used for mending nets and baiting lines and the surrounding cottages gave some protection from the weather.

THE HERRING SHEDS

By the 1840s the area bounded by Crewe Street, South Street and Union Street was dominated by herring sheds and curing houses owned by John and Andrew Ewing. They were responsible for the majority of the 6000 barrels of herring shipped from the port in 1843-44 and, at one time, had a virtual monopoly of the trade. They employed gangs of "herring girls" to clean, gut and pack the fish into barrels of brine. It was an exhausting and repetitive job but they worked with such speed and dexterity that many of them earned as much as ten shillings (50p) per day. Since most of the "herring girls" followed the fishing fleets down the east coast as far as Yarmouth, their stay in Seahouses was often no more than two or three weeks. They catered for themselves and usually slept in makeshift dormitories above the herring sheds.

THE OLD SMOKEHOUSE

At the end of South Street on the left hand side of the road are the premises of Swallow Fish Ltd. This is now the only surviving smokehouse in Seahouses. It was built in the 1830s at the beginning of the herring boom. Swallow Fish still smoke herring and salmon but the fish are usually brought in by road from Scotland. To make kippers the herrings are first split,

The Seahouses terminus of the North Sunderland Railway c.1930. It is now the site of the car park and Tourist Information Office. The walk begins and ends here. (Courtesy of Alan Glenn).

soaked in a brine solution and then hung onto tenterhooks inside the smokehouse. Small fires of oak chippings burn on the floor and provide the smoke which cures and preserves the fish. These traditional kippers can be purchased from the small shop which was once used as a kitchen by the herring girls who slept in the dormitory above.

* Turn right from South Street and walk to the end of Union Street. Now cross the road to Chapel Lane. It is marked No. 6 on your map.

THE BLACK SWAN AND THE OLDE SHIP

The Black Swan and the Schooner Inn were both mentioned in the trade directories of Seahouses from the 1830s. The Black Swan was built about 1834 by Richard Hall who became one of Seahouses leading citizens. Hall acted as a grain merchant and shipping agent between 1835 and his death in 1865. In October 1838 he hosted the Dundee owners of the **Forfarshire** at the sale of materials salvaged from the shipwreck. The original name plate of the **Forfarshire** is displayed inside the pub.

As the path narrows at the entrance to Chapel Lane, notice the grooves cut into the sandstone coping on your right. They were made by generations of fishermen who used the coping stone to

sharpen their knives in order to prise open mussels and limpet shells. Continue along Chapel Lane as far as the Olde Ship Hotel on your right. The Olde Ship is one of Seahouses oldest surviving buildings and has been a public house since 1812. It was originally built as a farm house and the lintel of a doorway at the rear of the pub carries the date 1745. Inside, the Olde Ship has an extensive collection of memorabilia and nautical artefacts and is well worth a visit.

* From the Olde Ship cross the road and make your way back into Main street and the Car Park.

Your walk around Seahouses ends here, but remember there are a number of other walks and places of interest in the locality. You might wish to consider:

1. A walk into North Sunderland Village to view Railston House and an unusual whalebone arch in the grounds of the school.

2. A short drive to Bamburgh to view the castle and the lifeboat museum.

3. Moving on to the next walk described in this booklet — Berwick-upon-Tweed.

BERWICK AND BERWICK HARBOUR

by Francis Cowe

INTRODUCTION

Berwick was a thriving seaport during the early Middle Ages and a royal burgh of Scotland, but constant warfare in the Borders destroyed the prosperity of the town. Berwick was sacked and captured by the English in 1296, retaken by the Scots in 1318, surrendered to the English again after the Battle of Halidon Hill in 1333, only to be returned to Scotland in 1461. From 1482, however, Berwick was an English fortress on Scottish soil, forcibly detached from its natural hinterland. "This town", wrote Sir William Brereton in 1634, "... seems almost environed with the sea. The haven is a most narrow, shallow, barren haven, the worst that I have seen ... [but] it might be made good" ... Sir William Brereton's words were prophetic. By the beginning of the eighteenth century Berwick stood at the threshold of prosperity once again. Improved methods of cultivation in north Northumberland and the eastern Borders generated a significant agricultural surplus and Berwick soon became one of the principal grain ports in the Kingdom. In addition to grain and other agricultural products, ships came to Berwick for salmon and herring, paper from the Berwickshire mills and woollens from Hawick and Jedburgh. Merchants prospered and many of the fine houses and public buildings that now adorn the town were built from the profits that they made.

* The walk begins in the Bridge Street Car Park. Make your way to the steps at the rear of the car park. They lead up to the Quay Walls where the walk begins. It is marked No. 1 on your map.

THE QUAY WALLS AND SHOREGATE

The Quay Walls were rebuilt in the 1760s immediately in front of the medieval, riverside walls which now carry the footpath. They contain some of Berwick's finest Georgian houses; no. 13 was used as the Custom House between 1825 and 1917 and has recently been restored by the Town Preservation Trust.

Shoregate is one of the principal openings through the walls. It was formerly known as the Fish Gate and connects the streets of Hide Hill and Sandgate to the riverside. In Hide Hill, on the right, stands the Kings Arms Hotel, a former coaching inn, and there is another, the Hen and Chickens in Sandgate. The large turreted building, also on the right between the two coaching inns, was formerly the Corn Exchange built in 1858. It is now used as the municipal swimming pool. The Playhouse Cinema on the opposite side of the road was converted from a disused granary.

Guide map for walk

(© Crown Copyright)

TWEEDMOUTH, THE SALMON STATIONS AND THE BRIDGES

An ancient, low-water ford once ran between Shoregate and the opposite bank of the River Tweed close to Tweedmouth church as you view. The weather vane is made, appropriately, in the form of a salmon, since the best fisheries were on the south side of the river. One of the salmon stations, Gardo, is still worked in the old manner with coble and net. Tweedmouth and Berwick are now joined by three famous bridges which can be seen upstream, to the right. In the distance is the Royal Border Bridge designed by Robert Stephenson for the York, Newcastle and Berwick Railway in 1850. The ferro-concrete, Royal Tweed Bridge of 1928 is in the centre and in the foreground the pink-stoned, 15-arch Berwick Bridge completed in 1624.

The Tweed Dock, immediately opposite Shoregate on the south side of the river was opened in 1877 to accommodate the larger ships which were then using the river. The gates of the dock were removed and the entrance widened in 1993-94. Commercial shipping continues to use the Tweed Dock and the principal export is still grain.

* The walk continues along the Quay Walls to Coxon's Tower which is marked No. 2 on your map. As you walk, notice the imposing Customs House, with the royal arms above the doorway. It was built in the eighteenth century as a private dwelling and used as a Dispensary from 1826 to 1872. It has been used as the Custom House since 1917. A little further along, No. 21 Quay Walls is a striking and unusual Georgian House with venetian windows at first and second floor level. It was once the home of Thomas Sword Good (1789-1872), a talented local artist.

WELLINGTON TERRACE, THE SALUTING BATTERY AND COXON'S TOWER

As you approach Coxon's Tower, the path passes in front of three attractive houses which form Wellington Terrace. Numbers 1 and 2 were described as new in 1816; number 3 was built in 1852 as a church manse. The first house is of particular interest. It was built for John Miller Dickson, sailmaker, shipowner and manager of the Berwick Whaling Company. The door of the house is decorated with imitation harpoon heads. Notice also the stone flagged positions set into the grass on your right. This stretch of the Georgian walls was known as the Saluting Battery. There were originally positions for thirteen guns which could be fired through embrasures in the parapet at any enemy shipping foolish enough to enter the harbour.

Coxon's Tower is a look-out and defensive post at the far end

Tweed salmon was one of the staples of Berwick's trade. Here, the fishermen at the Gardo pose for the camera with their coble, nets and equipment about 1890. (Berwick Record Office).

of the Saluting Battery. It was built during the eighteenth century on the site of an earlier tower. Coxon's Tower is an excellent vantage point from which to view the Tweed estuary.

THE CARR ROCK AND THE LIFEBOAT HOUSE

On the opposite bank of the Tweed, at the river's edge, a short stone pier can be seen jutting into the river. The pier was built close to the site of the Carr Rock, which was once the only deep water anchorage in the River Tweed. It was chosen in 1807 as the anchorage for Berwick's two whaling ships, the **Lively** and the **Norfolk**, which sailed annually to the Arctic to hunt the Greenland Right Whale. The **Lively** was wrecked in the Davis Straits in 1825 but the **Norfolk** later became famous as one of the few whalers to survive two successive seasons icebound in the Arctic pack in 1835 and in 1836-37. The whalers usually entered the river and anchored at the Carr Rock at highwater. As the tide began to ebb their cargoes of blubber, stowed in barrels, were pitched overboard and allowed to float downstream to Spittal Point where they were recovered and processed into whale oil at a boiling house.

Just below the Carr Rock is the Lifeboat house, where the current rescue boat, the **Joy and Charles Beeby**, is housed. There has been a lifeboat stationed at Berwick since 1835.

* The walk continues along the Georgian walls from Coxon's Tower to Bay Terrace and the Pier Gate which is marked No. 3 on your map. The next battery on the walls is known as **Fisher's Fort** and displays a solitary Russian cannon captured during the Crimean War. Beyond the fort, on the left of the path, the long rectangle of grass known as the Avenue, was formerly used as a rope-walk during the eighteenth century. Rope making was an important local industry in the days of sailing ships and there were several roperies in Berwick and Tweedmouth.

BERWICK HARBOUR AND ITS SHIPPING

Berwick could be a difficult port for sailing ships to use. The harbour entrance is shallow and dangerously exposed to onshore winds, especially from the east and south east. Moreover, there are strong tides in the river especially after periods of heavy rain. The pier which was built between 1810 and 1821 gives some protection from northerly winds. It was built on the site of several earlier structures. The lighthouse was added in 1826.

Most of the vessels trading from Berwick were small coasters. Only 15 of the 57 vessels registered at the port in 1825-26 exceeded 100 tons and the average size of all vessels was 88

Berwick from Carr Rock

At one time the Carr Rock was the only deep water anchorage in the River Tweed. The Berwick whalers operated from here between 1807-37. In this view a top-sail schooner discharges its cargo, while two large square-riggers await to load. On the right a smaller coasting smack lies moored in the stream. (Berwick Record Office).

Topsail schooners at the Carr Rock c.1880. (Courtesy of Francis Cowe).

tons. Not surprisingly the two Greenland whalers were the largest ships at the port in 1825, although the Berwick smacks were undoubtedly the best known. Developed for the carriage of salmon to the London market, the smacks acquired a considerable reputation as passenger ships because of their speed, reliability and cheapness. Even the worst of winter weather rarely held them up for long and few were ever shipwrecked. There were 20 smacks sailing from the port in 1806 with names like the **Tweed Packet, Neptune** and **Britannia.**

As you look towards the pier the large industrial buildings on the left of Pier Road were built as granaries in or soon after 1837. They are now owned by the firm of William Leith, tentmaker, which is the direct descendant of John Miller Dickson's sailmaking business. Beyond the pier there are some spectacular views to the south where the bulky outlines of Holy Island and Bamburgh Castles can normally be seen.

* From Pier Gate the path ascends Kipper Hill, where the former herring curing house with its pantiled roof can be seen on the left. The walk leaves the Elizabethan walls by a narrow footpath to the left. Notice the garrison magazine building of 1749 on the right and the Lions Gardens, cultivated allotments on your left. The gardens occupy the site of another eighteenth century rope works. In front is the

Lions House, built for John Turner Curry, a Berwick freeman and ship's master, in 1809. The path descends by steps into Ravensdowne. It is marked No. 4 on your map.

RAVENSDOWNE AND THE ICE-HOUSES

The house immediately to your left on entering Ravensdowne was originally constructed as three separate cottages in 1797. In 1978-79 the cottages were renovated and converted into a single dwelling by the Town Preservation Trust. The buildings attached to this house, fronted by a high wall which is topped with ivy, were originally designed and used as ice-houses. Ice gathered from local ponds or brought in by ship from Norway, was stored in ice-houses like these during the winter months. During the summer it was used for the preservation of salmon on their carriage to market. Refrigeration was first practised in Berwick in 1788 and there were, in the early nineteenth century, six commercial ice-houses in different parts of the town.

* From Ravensdowne the walk continues along Woolmarket, across the top of Hide Hill and into Marygate in the centre of the town. Marygate is Berwick's principal thoroughfare and market place. The Town Hall, on the right, was built between 1750 and 1761. It is open to the public and well

worth a visit. The spire of the Town Hall is still used as a leading mark by ships approaching the harbour. Leave Marygate by the first turning on the left, which is called Eastern Lane and make your way to the Maltings. It is marked No. 5 on your map.

THE MALTINGS AND EASTER WYND

The Maltings is Berwick's Arts Centre and was opened in 1990. It was originally constructed, as its name suggests, as a granary. The interior of the old building was destroyed by fire in 1984, but the thick walls, built to withstand the heavy floor loadings of bulk grain storage, were undamaged and allowed the conversion of the building to its present use. The building opposite the Maltings, on the right, is known as Easter Wynd and is another example of the alteration of a former granary, this time into dwellings. The original grain store was built in the first half of the eighteenth century and subsequently extended several times.

Below the Maltings, the newly formed Shoe Lane runs off to the left and down to a pleasant courtyard. At the rear of the yard the high wall of the Arts Centre reveals the sheer size of the former granary.

* Follow Shoe Lane down to and across Bridge Street into

Sallyport which can be recognised as a narrow passage entered through an arch from Bridge Street. It is marked No. 6 on your map.

BRIDGE STREET, SALLYPORT AND GRANARIES

Before entering Sallyport pause to look at the buildings in Bridge Street which is one of Berwick's oldest thoroughfares. It is full of interesting buildings that contained shops below and merchants houses above. Many of the yards behind these buildings were used by coopers who made the barrels or kitts in which salmon and other fish were packed for carriage to market.

Sallyport was constructed as a narrow passage through the Walls, by which members of the garrison could make a sudden attack against an enemy besieging the town. Halfway through the lane, on the left, the heavily buttressed walls of Dewar's Lane granary come into view. The granary was built sometime after 1815 on the site of an earlier grain store which was destroyed by fire. The building is derelict and its future uncertain.

To the right, at the same halfway point in Sallyport, the work of the Preservation Trust presents a sharp contrast. Here, two extensive properties — one a shop and house in Bridge Street and the other a granary on Quay Walls — have been given a new lease of life. The granary building has been converted into flats and offices, but its original form, with fine rubble stonework and windows with brick arches and sills, can clearly be seen. The rear of the granary, which includes an interesting brick chimney, can normally be seen in the courtyard beyond the first range.

* Now make your way onto the Old Town Quay, which can be reached from the courtyard by a narrow passage through the walls or by following Sallyport. In both passages the contrast between the medieval and Georgian stonework can be seen. Walk along the quay to the Little Dock which is marked No. 7 on your map.

THE TOWN QUAY AND ITS TRADE

In recent years Berwick Quay has been deserted by shipping and in places it lay in ruins. Most of the buildings that were placed on it have also been removed. In 1993-94, however, a major rescue operation was undertaken and the oldest section, from Berwick Bridge to the Little Dock, was piled with steel girders to keep the river out.

The original, medieval quayside, was much closer to Bridge Street and, through the centuries, has slowly advanced into the Tweed. There is good archaeological evidence to suggest that it began as a series of private quays or wharves, each connected with a merchant's dwelling and warehouse on the south side of Bridge Street. But when the riverside section of the town wall was built during the fourteenth century the quay had to be rebuilt outside it. Until the eighteenth century the quay was small — no more than 100 yards in length — but it was gradually extended towards Shoregate. The Georgian Town Walls are pierced by several openings onto the Quay, most of which led into commercial buildings on the other side. The first of them is a small studded door which marks the Quayside entrance to the Dewar's Lane granary. Grain was delivered to the Quay by means of small waggons which used a narrow gauge railway. Part of the iron rails can still be seen behind the door. Almost all of the trade which passed through the port before 1850 was handled at the Quay. When the harbour was busy and the Quay could not accommodate all the ships waiting to use it, some of them tied up at dolphins in the river or used mooring rings on the piers of Berwick Bridge.

In the third week of January 1760, for example, 8 vessels sailed from the port and the same number arrived. On 23 January, the **Isabella,** Alexander Henderson master, sailed for Leith with wheat and barley as the **Otter,** Joseph Bull, arrived from London with a general cargo of sugar, molasses, rum, tobacco

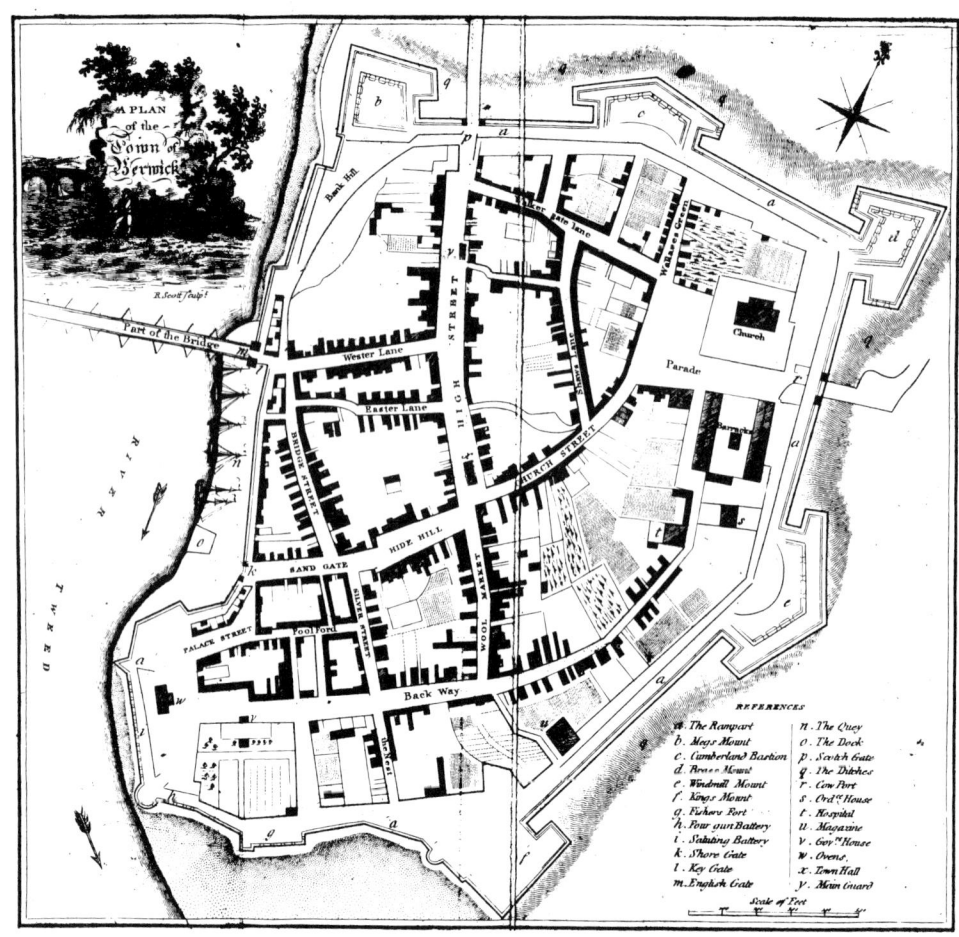

Quayside detail from map of 1799. (Reproduced from Fuller's History of Berwick).

and assorted sacks of seeds, hops and other goods. The cargo of the **Samuel and Christian**, Charles Miller master, which sailed for London on 26 January in company with several other vessels, was almost identical to those carried later by the Berwick smacks — chests of eggs, kitts of salmon, tubs of pork and bags of grain. In its heyday Berwick Quay was the scene of almost constant noise and movement.

THE LITTLE DOCK AND THE CHANDLERY

At one time the upstream wall of the Little Dock formed the end of the Town Quay but, in an extension constructed about 1750, a new stone wall was built to enclose the dock area. The stonework tells the story clearly — the newer wall is constructed from bevelled stones. The old steps in the upstream wall of the dock end abruptly half way down the wall. They were probably constructed as embarkation steps for passengers using the Berwick smacks, and could be used at any state of the tide.

The building known as the Chandlery, recently restored, was yet another granary. It was later used as a sail loft. On the other side of the Chandlery, there is a slipway which marks the site of one of Berwick's oldest shipyards. Arthur Byram began a ship building business close-by in 1751 and it was run by his descendents, generally with great success, until 1878. The yard was revived after the Second World War but is derelict again although the slipway is still used for repairing boats.

* The walk leaves the Quay by way of Shoregate. Bridge Street Car Park is immediately on your left after you pass through the gate.

Your walk around Berwick ends here, but there are a number of others you might wish to consider.

1. Along the riverside upstream from the top of Love Lane. This walk leads to the remains of Berwick Castle.

2. A complete tour of the Town Walls.

3. A visit to the Town Hall in Marygate, the museums at the Barracks on the Parade and Holy Trinity Church, which is opposite the Barracks.

FURTHER READING

If you would like to find out more about the history of these three ports then the following books may be of interest. Although some of them are out-of-print, it is possible to request them from your local library.

ALNMOUTH

Dickson, W — Four chapters from the history of Alnmouth, G Bouchier Richardson, 1852.

Graham, P A — Highways and Byways in Northumbria, Spreddon Press, 1988.

Hickes, J C — The History and Development of Lesbury and Alnmouth, Alnwick Gazette, nd.

Northumberland County History Committee — A History of Northumberland, Vol II, A Reid, 1893.

BERWICK-UPON-TWEED

Cowe, F M — Berwick-upon-Tweed. A short historical guide, Bells Bookshop (printed by Tweeddale Press Ltd), 1975.

Fuller, J — The history of Berwick-upon-Tweed, 1799. (Reprint F Graham, published by The Scolar Press Limited, Menston, Yorkshire 1973).

Gordon, L — Berwick-upon-Tweed and the East March, Phillimore, 1985.

Lamont-Brown, R — The Life and Times of Berwick-upon-Tweed, John Donald, Edinburgh, 1988.

Scott, J — Berwick-upon-Tweed. The History of the town and Guild, Elliot Stock, London, 1888.

SEAHOUSES

Graham, F — Northumbria's Lordly Strand, F Graham, 1974.

Grierson, E — The Companion Guide to Northumbria, Collins, 1976.

Northumberland County History Committee — A History of Northumberland, Vol I, A Reid, 1893.

Northumberland Federation of Womens Institutes — The Northumberland Village Book, Countryside Books, Newbury and NFWI Newcastle, 1994.

THE AUTHORS

Tony Barrow was born at Sedgefield, County Durham, in 1947 and graduated from Newcastle University in 1970. He has taught History in Secondary and Further Education ever since. Tony is well known to many local history societies and family history groups in the region for his illustrated talks and lectures and is the author of numerous articles about aspects of the maritime history of Northumberland and Durham. He received his doctorate in 1989 for research into the North East Coast Whale Fisher 1750-1850. Tony is currently Head of History in the Department of Humanities and Science at Newcastle College.

David Bond was born at Wallsend in 1955. After leaving school he worked in various jobs in local shipyards and engineering firms. After he was made redundant in 1982, David became a mature student at Newcastle College and later graduated from Newcastle Polytechnic with a BA (Hons) in English and History in 1986. He has taught History and Information Technology in various colleges of further education and is now Principal Archives Education Officer for Hampshire County Council.

Francis Cowe is a native of Berwick. He is widely consulted for his extensive knowledge of the local history of the town and the surrounding area. Some of his studies of the Berwick smacks and the trade that they carried have been published locally and he is the author of **Berwick-upon-Tweed: A Short Historical Guide.**